What School Never Taught My Daughter:

A Financial Literacy Note for Teens

Talent Tarisai Manyonga

First published in Harare, 2021.

ISBN: 978-1-77920-752-4

Published by: RuvaraShe Everblooming Publishers

(+263773868946/+263719868946)

Copyright © Talent Tarisai Manyonga

What School Never Taught my Daughter: A Financial Literacy Note for Teens

All rights reserved. No part of this publication may be reproduced, stored in a retrieval system, or transmitted in any form or by any means, electronic, mechanical, photocopying, recording or otherwise, without the prior permission of the publisher and the author.

Editor: Tendai Chinhoro
Cover Design: Francis Chidavaenzi

Printed in Harare, Zimbabwe.

ACKNOWLEDGEMENTS

While writing a book might sound an individual activity, being a woman and a social being, there are a lot of relationships that interfere with the activity. So as a wife, a mother, a sister, a daughter-in-law, an aunt, et cetera, I know many times I willingly or unwillingly did not attend to those relationships as expected of me. May I be forgiven; it was not by design.

While I cannot mention everyone by name, I feel highly indebted not to mention people like my husband, Walter Chigwada for all the support. Sometimes I would wake him up in the middle of the night to share an idea as the book was developing. Apologies for that and thank you for being lovingly there for me. I also want to acknowledge Tendai Chinhoro for helping me in bringing the literary flavor to the contents of the book and to put it in the narrative form. I wanted to make the book a bit more interesting to read to teenagers, my target audience, than a textbook would offer and Tendai helped me a lot in that regard. Tabeth Ruvarashe Manyonga, my sister, thank you for the assistance you gave me in the publishing process of the book. I am your older sister, but you experienced the publishing journey first. As I was writing, I knew when the time to publish this book would come, you were going to show me the way since you already had published works of your own. Thank you for inspiring me and walking with me to this point. To my parents Cowen and Dorothy Manyonga, thank you for all the support and believing in my idea from the day I called you to share the idea with you and I hope that the book will still make you feel proud of me. Last but not least, I want to mention the unwavering support my cousin Happiness Manyonga gave me. Nothing beats the gift of encouragement to someone. Thank you very much.

DEDICATION

To my two rainbow children, Tavimbanashe and Kunashe. At six and three years of age respectively you are still young but mom has decided to put on paper what she always teaches you about money into a book so that in her absence you will still have her words in print. One day you will be teenagers and this gift will be waiting for you. May the Lord protect you as you grow in wisdom and the power of discernment.

To my late Uncle, Esau Manyonga, the little girl you named Talent many years ago is now living one of the talents. You told me you named me Talent because you saw a special and talented someone in me. Thank you for seeing in me what others could not see. Your words of encouragement were seeds you sow in me and with this book the world can now see them germinating. I hope wherever you are, you are happy I have grown to become a writer. May you continue to rest in eternal peace.

And most importantly to every teen, and every reader who is going to read this book, may the insights transform your money perceptions and give you so much control over each dime you get hold of.

CONTENTS

Prologue — vii

Chapter 1: Values and Beliefs — 1

Chapter 2: Re-shaping money memory lane — 17

Chapter 3: How to start earning income with no capital — 23

Chapter 4: What to do with the money you make in your teens — 32

Chapter 5: Budgeting as a teen: Grow your money while you're young — 39

Chapter 6: Epilogue — 48

PROLOGUE

My Dearest Daughter

Once again, I want to say Happy Birthday to you! May God bless you with more years.

Over the years at your birthday, apart from the traditional cake, I have been buying you different material things. Looking at you now, I am happy to see how you have blossomed into a big girl who is gradually but surely moving towards the worlds of adulthood and womanhood. I, as your mother have shared with you various issues about life but we have rarely talked about money and money life. You have been to school where you have received countless lessons in all those fifteen subjects you always pass with flying colours but still I feel that what you are getting in school is not enough to prepare you for financial prudence. Today you have turned fifteen and you have a whole long life ahead of you and I don't want that long life to be a financially miserable one. I am not saying the words in this long letter will be all you need to know all your life for you to be able to carry yourself through the mazes of financial struggles but I am sure from them you will be able to have a reference tool. My words will be your drawing board from which you will always come back and see where you will have gone wrong.

I am not sure whether I know and understand what you believe in and value as a person. As I watch you grow, what I am seeing and know about you could be just a tip of who you really are, no matter you being my daughter. Whatever the values and beliefs you have acquired over these years I am sure they have also extended in the way you see money and ultimately this has become part of your personality. In school you have been taught Accounting, Economics, Management of Business and Commerce. At church they have taught you how to live with or without people and perhaps what it means to be a born-again woman in spiritual and social terms but in both scenarios, there has never been a subject dedicated to money. I have therefore decided to fill in that gap as your mother. You must really count yourself blessed for receiving this lesson at fifteen. Personally, I only got to understand the basics of how money works in my early thirties and you can imagine the money errors I had made before that as a young woman.

I don't want you to be like the majority of people who manage their money without giving much thought to either what they are doing or why they are doing it. I want you to have power over the way you spend or save your money, whatever amount God blesses you with at any given time. I want you to always be satisfied with your financial status at any given time. My letter will be long and therefore I will put it in chapters, topics and sub-topics and I will start with the topic of values and beliefs.

Chapter 1

Values and Beliefs

I want to tell you what money personality, values and beliefs are as well as the different types of money personalities. This will assist you to understand your relationship with money as an individual.

As your mother, growing up I thought financial success had something to do with luck. Like how you might have referred to those who seem to flow financially as 'the lucky ones'. This later turned out to be wrong as I grew older. There is hardly any magic or the work of an unforeseen force called luck when it comes to financial success. Rather it is all closely related to our money personalities. The unique part of us that guides our interaction with money determines how far we can go with it. It is all in our values and beliefs regarding money; and can be influenced by one's attitude, expectations and emotions. I wouldn't want to one day, when I am gone, turn in my grave on the realization that I raised a daughter who doesn't place any value in money, a daughter whose beliefs and attitude in money are undesirable. Against this background, I want you from today onwards to be aware of what you value and believe so that you won't consistently make poor financial decisions but successful ones. You will only be able to do this if you don't draw from the same value set and beliefs for each transaction you make. Whether you like it or not, your values and beliefs about money will be the driving forces behind your spending habits. They are constructed from life experiences with money and have an intertwined and profound effect on your financial behavior. This long letter, my daughter, is a summary of my own life experiences which I'm trying to bestow unto you as well, so that they become part of your money personality.

The most important value I want to inculcate in you and which you must make part of you is that of having security belief in money. For if you believe that there is security in money, you will be able to save it. However, there are values and beliefs which I pray will never take root in you. The belief that money brings you respect. Firstly, as a human being and secondly as a woman, you must know things that bring you respect. Definitely it's not money. If you fall into the trap of this deceiving 'value' you will end up spending money on expensive material things like clothes, cars, and other unnecessary status symbols.

The same misleading value that tells you respect is earned through flashy material things is the same value that will lead you to think that happiness results from spending a lot of money. This will only let you continually spend excessively in the pursuit of happiness. When you turn eighteen, I will write another letter on what gives you happiness and what earns you respect as a woman. I promise.

As I mentioned earlier, a value is something that is very important and desirable to the one who holds it and it influences how they spend their time, energy, and money. One striking characteristic about values again which 1 am worried about and which have spurred me to pen this long letter to you is that values reflect one's upbringing and are influenced by historic events and people in one's life including family, peers, teachers, coaches, neighbors, church leaders and the community as a whole. While all these people have a role to play but, when things go wrong, the world will point fingers at the mother. Your peers are mostly like you, their minds are blank slates in terms of money matters. Your teachers were not trained to teach you money life, church leaders are also busy with our spiritual lives. Everything therefore squarely falls on me, your closest friend from pre-birth up to now. I will never tire.

I know as you will be growing you will not only have just one value but many of them. Since these values are all important, it is also important that you prioritize them so that you can be able to choose between two or more competing values in certain situations. I saw you when you were growing. There is this sense in you to value friendship. You have also been a straightforward girl in your deeds meaning to some extent you value an honest life. This means if a friend asks you to steal something, this will be a challenge to your value of leading an honest life. This means that you will have to decide whether you value honesty more than your friendship or vice versa. Obviously as your mother, I will challenge you to stand with honesty over friendship. Another example is that, if you value both looking very stylish in the latest fashions and financial security, you will have to decide which value is more important than the other. Again, if you base your 'spending values' on looking stylish, you may spend money freely in the name of fashion whenever something catches your eye. If you base your 'spending values' on financial security, you may be more likely to shop within a budget and practicing the principle of paying yourself first. When it comes to shopping you will go for 'for sale' items or may seek out discount outlet stores. I think you have seen how I do it when I buy clothes for you. I always make sure I buy less the same clothes others buy at high prices. I buy jackets and jerseys in September for a reason.

An idea someone holds to be true is called a belief. Like values, beliefs are also typically a result of life experiences and stem from information picked up along the way from family, friends, peers, the media and other channels. As you can see, I also hold myself highly responsible to what you will believe to be true in life. I don't want you to get into financial trouble because you built a set of wrong belief systems about money whilst I was living with you under the same roof. Financial trouble can occur when 'money beliefs' are based on what a person has heard or seen modelled, rather than based on facts (something that can be proven to be true). I want to believe that whatever life I have lived since you were born has been the best money behavior model. Be that as it may, I am not the only person that has influenced your beliefs and therefore my prayer is that you will have the power of discernment in seeing beyond the surface when anything falls on in the path of your money life.

One thing I also want you to note is that since beliefs can be subjective, they may be based on inaccurate 'facts', so it is important to verify whether beliefs are truly factual before acting on them. Some examples of beliefs that are not based on facts are:

- *You have to be lucky to have a lot of money.*

- *Being rich will make you happy.*

- *Borrowing is a good way of having money.*

- *Money is safest hidden under a mattress.*

- *Borrowing and not paying back here and there is not bad.*

I know that our money belief patterns are probably more negative and limiting than most areas of our lives. You have heard statements like, 'Money is not easy to make and keep, we just have to live each day as it comes'. Our culture portrays a picture of real love or hatred relationships with money. As a girl, I know the boundaries that you must create between lust for money and the value you give money. Lust for money will send you to gain it through unorthodoxy means. The money we are talking about here is the one you earn through orthodoxy ways. The money that rightfully belongs to you.

This kind of thinking might have already creeped in you, never mind you are just fifteen and I want you to have a re-alignment of your beliefs. I want you to look at money from this angle:

- Get rid of negative emotions and beliefs, insert new and positive beliefs.

- Create a compelling future by creating financial goals.

- Take action to your financial freedom.

- Remain focused on your desired outcome and reframe any obstacles to keep your unconscious mind moving forward.

Well, I know that as you will be growing from fifteen you will have many aspirations. From these I want you to aspire to improve your financial wellness and you will only be able to do this if you become aware of the role your financial attitudes and beliefs have in your future. As you will see beliefs help to explain key differences between savers, spenders, and those people who try to avoid money matters completely. Beliefs can be extremely stubborn and are difficult to change since they can become a part of our ongoing 'money script' or life story that follows our financial behaviors.

Never think I am inundating you with new terms that might upset you, my daughter, for if I don't mention them, the whole purpose of writing this letter will be lost. I will take my time to explain each money term I find you might need elaboration. Guess what? Blessed are you, for knowing these things at your age. While financial wellness starts early in life, many children of your age are not that lucky to have focused lessons on finance like the one I am giving you now. All they know is how to spend what their parents give them as pocket money and how to request for more.

The term 'money scripts' is used to describe financial beliefs that are often developed early in life and are frequently passed from one generation to the next. So, as you can see, whatever money script you show now is a direct result of what I, as your mother has so far offered in your life. No matter where you are on the journey to reaching your financial life goals, it's always helpful to be aware of your past experiences with money, whether they were positive or negative. I just hope that what you have engrained in yourself as a result of my modelling has been positive. I wouldn't want to blame myself for having waited too long to engage you on this important life lesson.

I know I am your mother but I'm giving you this chance to interpret your own life, the financial life you have lived this far as an individual or as part of the family. Just take a moment to answer these simple questions:

- What are some of your earliest money-related memories and experiences?
- Was money a frequent source of arguments or was the topic often avoided?
- What are your current 'money scripts' or financial belief patterns?

The four types of money beliefs

In writing this letter, allow me to quote some of the learned people who studied human beings and their money behaviors. I will start with a research performed by Dr. Brad Klontz and Dr. Sonya Britt, professors at Kansas State University, who found out that three out of four primary money beliefs (money avoidance, money status and money worship) are linked to potentially destructive financial behaviours. For example, these patterns of money beliefs have been associated with having lower levels of net worth, lower income, and higher amounts of debt. The other money belief, money vigilance, was not linked to problematic financial behavior.

Now as I said earlier, I will be taking time to elaborate on each of these terms. I was patient enough from the day I conceived you and saw every moment of you as you were growing from birth. It has been my duty to pay attention to every detail about you. Let me, therefore, take time to explain the various money types as discovered by the researchers I mentioned above.

Money Avoiders

In general, money avoiders tend to view money as negative and a source of fear, anxiety, or disgust and often have beliefs that wealthy individuals are greedy. Money avoiders think that they don't deserve money or that money is bad and the root of all evil. In addition, they also tend to believe that it's not okay to accumulate more wealth during your lifetime than you will actually need. Money avoiders may experience conflicting beliefs that having more money and wealth could improve their life satisfaction, self-worth and social status. This belief system can create a tug-of-war between feelings of contempt towards money and wealthy individuals to placing too much emphasis and value on the role of money during their life journeys. At this point I want to point out that the emphasis of this letter is not to make you a money worshipper for the Bible has taught us the lust for money is the beginning of all evil. But always remember that there is a difference between lust for money and cherishing the existential power of having money in your life. Who is a money worshipper?

Money Worshippers

Money worshippers believe that having more money will solve all their problems and money is the key to happiness. Now my daughter as I said earlier, money alone without other virtues necessary for human growth won't give you happiness and a sense of fulfilment in your life. Equally all other things being there minus money will make your life miserable. I wouldn't want you to become a miserable and poor virtuous woman, for this will only expose you to predators. Back to money worshippers.

These people have an associated money script that 'things will get better in life if I just have more money'. Another common belief is that the accumulation of more money will lead to increased happiness and overal life satisfaction. For the money worshipper, money is viewed as a scarce resource and there will never be enough of it. But as young as you are, you may ask, "How much more money does a rich person want?" You won't get an answer to that from a money worshipper. Money worshippers may prioritize work over family and social relationships. Now as I said money can only bring you happiness as part of other facets of life that make up a human being, including the social aspect of life. Sacrifice it over money and you will live an unhappy life. God willingly, when I marry you off one day, it will be to a human being not to money.

Money Status

People with money status belief systems tend to define their self-worth by their financial net worth. They also place a great deal of emphasis on buying the hottest new items with leading brand names and quality. Money is a sign of success for those with strong money status beliefs. As a result, these individuals may pretend to possess more wealth than they actually have and may overspend to provide others with an impression they have achieved financial success. I don't want you to fall in this category while I'm alive. I hope I will be able to inculcate in you some sense of vigilance in money which I'm going to explain next.

Money Vigilance

Money vigilance is typically associated with themes of frugality and people with these money beliefs tend to focus on the importance of saving, use discretion when discussing financial matters and express anxiety about not saving enough for emergencies. Money vigilant people are most likely to pay attention to their financial well-being. A common belief for the money vigilant is that people should work hard for their money and not expect financial handouts. They also tend to be more anxious and guarded when discussing money matters with people outside of their closest network of friends and family.

Now I know at fifteen you are still young, but you already have certain beliefs as well as life goals. Do the little money beliefs you have, support your life goals or they are likely to be a hinderance or not? However, I want to point out that some of these money beliefs are not always problematic because to some extent they can motivate us to keep focused on irking for survival so they may even be encouraged. It's only when we exercise them at the extremes were these money beliefs can cause problems. As I always tell you, too much of everything is not good. For now, lets look at how certain money beliefs can affect our behaviors.

Money worship beliefs

If you become one of the people with money worshipping beliefs you will become a person with compulsive spending, you will have work-life imbalances and hoarding behaviours. These beliefs can also be associated with financial dependence, giving money to others you cannot afford to part with and ignoring or not paying attention to one's own financial situation.

Money status beliefs

Money status beliefs are associated with compulsive spending problems and being financially dependent on others. Money status beliefs may also lead to secret spending or financial infidelity.

Money avoider's belief

If you become a money avoider you will have trouble setting life financial goals and struggle to stick to a personal spending plan or budget. This money belief is also linked with overspending and compulsive buying. Not surprisingly, money avoiders have difficulty organizing their finances and frequently struggle discussing money matters.

Money vigilant beliefs

Money vigilant beliefs can help you provide wealth protection. My prayer everyday is that you may have this type of money belief.

So, these are the money scripts which you will possibly become or which you will interact with. I am also sure you have noticed whom I want you to become. The beliefs that I want to take root in you. You are just fifteen and even if you were thirty, thirty-five or forty, it's never too late to rewrite your money script. It is however more advantageous to know these things at an early age. This is what I am trying to do to you. The good news, however, in life is that you have the opportunity to rewrite these money scripts. While money beliefs can be passed on from one generation to another, they do not have to be permanent. Perhaps, what I am telling you right now will have changed by the time you become thirty or so. You can always adapt, for as long as it leaves you in the desirable category. Once you have identified your patterns of thinking about money, you can begin to examine how changing those beliefs can fundamentally improve your financial situation. You will then truly be ready to take mindful, deliberate steps to turning resolutions of change into reality.

Chapter 2

Re-shaping money memory lane

We are going to move on to what I have termed re-shaping the money memory lane. At fifteen you have already lived a life that has given you certain beliefs and values about money. In this part of my letter, I want to share some money tips which I think your future self will be thankful for. You will also thank me.

As a teenager, you are in a very powerful position. Starting good money habits now will put you ahead for the rest of your life. Here are five money tips for you. If you decide to share them with your friends, it will still be fine. I wouldn't want you to be the only one equipped while your circle of friends will be ignorant. Personally, I was not good with money when I was a teenager. I used to spend it on stuff like clothes and eating at Eastgate Harare which was my favorite hanging place. It was like an all-in-one place. If I knew as a teenager even a fraction of what I know now about money, I'd probably be retired. So, let me help you avoid the mistakes I made with money by giving you the following five money tips.

Understand the power of time.

You probably aren't making any money right now, but that doesn't matter. What matters is time and your money has a lot in it. You need to start valuing every minute. Instead of wasting time on social media, going through people's profiles, admiring them, I urge you to use that time wisely either studying or researching how you can make money. If you notice here at home, we don't really watch TV, when we do so, it will be on educational channels.

Develop a money saving habit

How long have you been brushing your teeth? You're now a teenager which means it's been quite a long time; and because you have been doing it for so long, it has become a habit. The power of habit is almost as important as the power of time when it comes to money. A habit is just something you do involuntarily; you don't have to think about it too much. If you start the habit of saving money now, that habit will always be with you. Every dollar you get, whether it's a gift, an allowance or pay from a job, get into the habit of saving a portion of it. Half of it would be ideal and now is the time to start because you don't have a lot of expenses. The older you get, the harder it can seem to save even 10% of your money but if you start saving much more than that at an early age, it will not seem hard to you because it will have become a habit.

I remember one scenario when you were six years old, I tried to teach you financial literacy, but I guess you were still too young to grasp the concept. I gave you a R5 and instructed you on how to spend it but you did it your way. The instruction was for you not to spend all the money but to ask for change and bring it back home, to put in your saving jar. It took you four times to understand this concept. I was excited when you came rushing after school saying, *"mama today l brought change"*. Though it was just sixty cents, but l was happy you were now understanding the concept of not spending all what you have.

Get Educated

As I said in the beginning, you probably aren't getting much education about personal finance in school, maybe none at all. I have a whole conspiracy theory built around this. For example, the more you know about money, the less you are tied to a job for decades making money for someone else and the less consumer crap you buy. You can see that it's in the interest of certain groups to keep you in the dark when it comes to handling money. They don't control what you decide to do with your time and the lessons I'm telling you now. Reading personal finance books is a good start. Tell me which finance books have you read from the bookshelf? If none, this letter is your first finance resource and hopefully it will give you the hunger to read more books on the subject.

Talk to me as your parent about money. Some families don't like to talk about money, they think it's rude or a taboo or just none of their children's business. They are wrong because that kind of attitude is the reason why so many people leave home without any clue about how to handle money or anything related to it. You don't have to poke in my bank balances to have a discussion about money. You can speak and ask questions, in general terms. I don't remember you asking me anything to do with money. One of the best ways you could have used if you ever wanted to was to open the conversation and ask for the most important piece of money advice, I could give you. As parents we love to give advice and asking such open-ended questions can help to start a deeper conversation. At least, now you know it's an area I'm very much comfortable to share with you.

Make smart decisions about University

While I promise that as long as I'm alive I will always be there for all your life needs, including education you still need to make smart decisions about college. This can include the decision to attend a college where you are able to do part time job or work, so that you can assist in your tuition fees. A smart decision might mean applying for every grant and scholarship you are remotely qualified for. A smart decision is also choosing to major in something that people actually get paid to do. Career development is important. If you are not very careful, crippling yourself with a debt that can almost never be discharged is going to colour the rest of your life.

Avoid FOMO

FOMO stands Fear of Missing Out. It's easy to think everyone is having more fun than you when you're a teenager. Surely, sometimes people will be having more fun than you. That's true no matter how young or old you are. It's important, though, to not give up what you want most for what you want now. What you want now is to take care of the money you make from the little piece work you do here and there or from the pocket money I give you. What you want most is a debt free life; or to retire at forty instead of sixty-five or to be able to quit a job you hate because you have a big emergency fund to see you through to your next job. It might not seem like it right now being in your teens, but all of that will be true as you celebrate more birthdays. Is it really still early?

If you ask people older than you what their biggest financial regret is, a lot of them will tell you that they wished they had started getting serious about money much earlier than they did. I have already testified my regrets. This is so because, doing it only gets harder the older you get. Start now so you don't have that same regret a few decades down the road. The earlier you start the better. In all this remember, mom will always be there for you.

Chapter 3

How To Start Earning Income With No Capital

I know that earning money as a teenager can seem like an uphill struggle. Some teenagers are privileged they can have what they want because their parents are rich. Here, I'm talking of an economically average teenager. I don't know whether I have made you look like a rich daughter or an average one but in whatever scenario you find yourself in, my words are still relevant.

As a teenager, you also have more things to pay for such as; clothes, entertainment, food, outings with your friends as well as transport costs. As life gets more expensive, you are probably looking for ways to fund these expenses beyond the little pocket money I give you here and there. What I am trying to explain is that as a person you need to become productive for your own financial upkeep. Luckily, there are many ways for teens to earn money. The bottom line is it a great idea to start earning money as a teenager. When you take home your first pay slip, you'll likely have a big smile on your face. If you choose to make smart money moves with your teenage pay slip, then you'll enjoy greater financial stability later in life. However, as a teenager, you have to deal with your fair share of pressure. School demands, extracurricular activities and many more. The million-dollar question is, how are you supposed to find time to make any money? I get it completely no young person wants to beg for money from their parents all the time. Whether it's a basic job at our company, something part-time or starting your own business, there are countless ways to make money.

Some of these jobs might not sound appealing and don't make lots of money overnight but they teach you lasting lessons. Here are some ways to make money that you may need to explore. Yes, I'm giving them to you. You never saw that coming, right? Well, I said it's high time I went real with you. It's a woman-to-woman kind of talk. If I keep seeing you as a kid, at fifteen, I will still have a kid when you turn eighteen so, this is the time. Here are a few good jobs which you can try out as a teenager:

Start a blog.

A blog can be a fun way to earn extra money. You can blog about any topic that interests you. I know you like music and dancing so that can be your starting point. Blogging is not an easy way to earn an income, but it can be enjoyable. It may take several months to years before your blog earns a single cent, but it will definitely be a lucrative income once you get the ball rolling. Be prepared to create regular content for a growing audience. As your mother, I wish I had known of this earlier than now. I started blogging this year and I haven't started earning from it. I do enjoy writing about finances and imparting my knowledge to others, just as I have started doing to you. I know in few years to come this blog will generate income. You just need to define your niche. If you would like to know more on how to start a blog let me know and I will help you develop it.

Tutor younger kids

If you have excelled in a certain subject, then it is time to put those book smarts to the test. Many parents search high and low for a tutor that can help their kid make it through a class. If you have expertise in a particular area, then market that to the neighborhood. I'm so much comfortable with this one.

From tomorrow onwards, as you start eating into your sixteenth year since birth, I want you to do your research and check with parents in this area if they need a tutor for their children. When it grows, you can also hang up posters around town if you want to generate wider interest. As you start to hear from potential clients, make sure to talk to me and your dad and we will see how we can support you, especially in terms of space. Don't worry about our consent, you already have it. You can also make use of social media to advertise yourself.

Babysit

Babysitting is a common way for teenagers like you to earn money. A good place to start your babysitting activities is through family or friends. If you do a good job, then they can spread the word around the community. You might be surprised how much you can earn as a reliable babysitter. A typical rate is at least $2 per day plus an extra $1 for each additional child. Plus, most parents provide a meal to the babysitter. I know at fifteen you are still growing and you enjoy eating. Nevertheless, always remember mom will always have plenty of food for you in the house, right!

Another opportunity similar to babysitting is a parent helper. The parent would be home while you are helping out around the house. That might include anything from entertaining the kids to folding laundry. It can be a good first step if you aren't quite ready to watch a houseful of kids on your own. Remember, all this won't make you a housemaid, in case you might wonder what mom is driving you to.

Start a photography or video editing business

Well, I know you are a girl and some of these ideas might be inclined to boys but as your mother, I have never looked at careers or businesses with the lenses of sex and its limitations. I believe you can do what you feel is right for you my daughter. Like now if you feel you can be good at photographing or video editing, you can make some money from that. Many people will be constantly on the search for your services, especially if they know that it's a girl who is doing such a business with excellence. Have you ever seen how people look amazed when they see a woman driving a bus or a truck? That's the same issue. A woman who breaks through the fields dominated by men is usually highly regarded. You can offer to take pictures of an event or edit photos taken by the client. Video editing would be very similar.

Wash cars

Still sounding a boys' job, right? As I said I don't care you are a girl. Cars can be a big investment. Many people don't have time to keep their cars clean. A great idea could be to start up a neighborhood car washing service especially during the summer. You will be able to charge more if you bring your services to the customer. As long as the customer has water, then you should be able to take your services anywhere. As for the soaps, rags, and any other cleaning machines, don't worry, mom will make those ones available for you if you are interested.

Teach kids how to code

Coding is a valuable skill. If you already know how to code, then you can earn a significant amount of money teaching younger kids how to code. Many parents are willing to pay top dollar for their children to learn this skill. Coding is the process of using a programming language to get a computer to behave how you want it to. Every line of code tells the computer to do something and a document full of lines of code is called a script. Each script is designed to carry out a job. This job might be to take an image and change its size.

Making money through social media

You are only fifteen and some of the ideas that might make you money need a bit of someone who is older. I'm only telling you now because I feel its a critical opportunity to pour it out to you. When you turn eighteen or when you become a big lady, you will remember these words and perhaps you will still start something with this letter as the reference document, in case I might not be there for you. If you think you can be a social media expert who is always in tune with the latest trends, you put that interest to use and make money off it.

Social media is an excellent place to start if you want to make some quick cash. While watching your favorite cartoon, comedies or vlogs on YouTube, do you ever wonder how possible it is to make money on YouTube? If, your content is engaging enough and if you talk about topics people care about, YouTube can be a good revenue source.

You can also become a social media consultant, offering your services to smaller businesses to help them gain followers. If you're familiar enough with social media outlets and advertising mediums, you can translate your knowledge into cash.

Be a salesperson

Do you have clothes you no longer wear, games you no longer play, or stuff you never really used? Instead of throwing them away, flip those items for profit. You never know who is in need of something that you otherwise found inconsequential. You can sell to your neighbors or go to places like Mupedzanhamo and sell them. Remember we always call it decluttering for money reasons.

Reason you should start earning an income as a teenager

My daughter don't ever be shy to look for money because money loves those who look for it. Stop procrastinating and start earning yourself some money. Search for your talent and purpose and start charging it.

Although you may not need to bring in a payslip, it is still a good idea. Whatever you will get, even if you spend most of your money on fun experiences or cute clothes, there is an opportunity to save. When you make the effort to save a part of your income, it will add up over time. The years will allow compounding interest to grow your money to new heights. It may seem like a small amount of money is not worth saving, but every little bit counts.

Now I have said some of the business ideas I think as a teenager you might want to venture into, there are perhaps some you might be aware of outside the ones I have mentioned, no problem. I will be waiting to hear from you what you will have decided to get into and I'm giving you a month to think about it. Remember, whatever you will choose, mom will be there for you.

Chapter 4

What To Do With The Money You Make In Your Teens

Earning money in your teens is exciting. However, it is important not to spend it all at once. Yes, it's ok to spend some of it on fun things while you enjoy high school. A small amount of savings can go a long way. Your future self will thank you if you try to save a piece of every income. As your mother I'm more concerned with cultivating a sense of saving in you more than the hustling to get money part. Reason being, you might be good at hustling but as long as your sense of saving is poor, you will remain in one place. You will not see the fruits of all the hustling. This is the reason why when you were young at six, I started teaching you to bring change even if it was a small amount.

How to get started on the saving habit

Separate spending money from savings

That's the first thing to do. However, though you will have stashed the money you will have made in a savings account, you might be tempted to spend that money if you've run out of cash but please, don't touch it! Your savings are for essentials and emergencies, not for more straightforward purchases like food and so on. The smart thing to do is to have a transaction account and a direct deposit account which you can access on demand. You can always start a student transaction account and put some of your money in it in case you don't want to keep too much cash on you. This way, your goals won't be conflicted. Savings accounts are created for the long haul while transaction accounts deal with your everyday needs. Always keep that in mind.

Five steps to saving for something you really want

It can be hard to save for your first big buy—especially when cash is limited but tell you what, it's not impossible. You just need a little patience and a plan. Here are some simple ideas to help you get that thing you've been dreaming about.

Find your magic number

I know you are pretty young and no matter how much I want you to save, I know as a girl you also want to move with time, to move with the trends, reasonably, though. Maybe you're itching to lay your hands on the latest tablet or a new play station. Do some research to find out exactly where you can get the best deal and how much it will cost. After that, see where mom might chip in. Once you know how much you'll need to cover, shoot for saving a little more than that to pay for any extras like a protective case for the tablet. If you're eyeing a bigger purchase, like your first car, ask me as your mother and your father as well to consider matching contributions, which could supercharge your savings. All we will be looking for in you is that sense of saving, that belief that one should save first before acquiring. It also shows how serious you are about your goal which could earn you extra points. It will make me age in grace, knowing I have a goal-oriented daughter.

Know what to set aside

Firstly, take your purchase amount and subtract any savings you already have set aside. Then, based on when you want to make your purchase, divide the remaining balance you need by the number of weeks until your purchase. That's how much you have to put away each week to meet your goal. If the numbers seem impossible, you might try to give yourself more time to save or find ways to increase your earnings or contributions from me and your dad, all you need to do is to present to us convincing figures. Always keep a photo of your goal on your phone or in your room where I know you are reading this letter from, right now. This will help you to remind yourself how happy you'll be when you reach it. It sounds cheesy but it helps when you're tempted by impulse buying of a new gaming app or that lip gloss.

Save without thinking about it

If you don't have any savings, this could be a good time to start converting your cash into hard currency. I can help you open a savings bank account. Always have a certain percentage you will commit to saving. That way, you'll have to take extra steps if you decide to withdraw money, curbing the urge to spend. By the time you need some cash, the impulse to buy those new shoes on sale, that cool headband or your third movie run of the week may have passed. In every little income you receive take a small portion to put to your savings. This way you can reach your goal without even feeling it.

Make some easy spending trade-offs

To get a good handle on where your money goes, keep a spending diary for a month or two. It could be as simple as writing down the cost of every purchase in a notebook, or you could use an app that tracks your spending. Once you get started, you may realise you like knowing where your money is being spent. You'll probably also notice that small amounts can add up to big dollars fast. Look at what you are spending your money on and see if you can cut out certain things that are less important compared to your bigger goal or replace any regular expenses with something cheaper.

I'll caution you though, being less invested with your money means you're less connected to it and thus you may spend more. By taking time to track receipts and write down purchases manually, you will be well-informed where all of your dollars are going and will end up being more cautious with your spending. Whenever you need a motivation boost, take a peek at the photo of your goal, or text me, your mom or your BFF for encouragement. It's good to have an accountability partner, it makes the saving goal easier than not having one.

Look for ways to make more money

Check your progress every couple of weeks. If you're not saving as quickly as you'd like, you might, offer to do more chores around the house or take on a big project at home, like getting the garden ready for a change of season or cleaning out the garage, in exchange for a bigger allowance. Yes, mom will reward you where she thinks you have done a task, she could have possibly paid someone to get it done. Look for another side hustle on the list I shared a few paragraphs above. You must always look into having multiple streams of income. Whatever your goal, reaching it will be sweeter because you figured out how to do it on your own. Plus, you'll have learned smart saving habits you can use for the rest of your life. Not bad.

Saving money as a teenager is hard, especially when you have friends who go about buying new clothes and going on weekend trips but it's doable. Who said you need a wealth of experience to bring in wealth?

Improvising helps as well as keeping distinct records tracking how much you spend. There are also benefits as a student that you can use to your advantage and you can even turn your hobbies into revenue makers as I said earlier on. Sounds fun, doesn't it? Start saving towards your future while your future is way ahead of you! Avoid mom's path, who waited a bit late to know these important life habits.

Chapter 5

Budgeting as a teen: Grow your money while you're young

Growing up is all about making tough decisions and the earlier you make them, the better your future will be. As a teen here's how to budget for yourself.

Being a teenager can be fun but there are those things called responsibilities that can make adolescence feel like a drag. It surely doesn't have to be like that. As a young and sometimes naive person, money can become as easy to spend as it is to make. Just like you see me and your dad doing, you have to learn how to budget your money as you handle growing responsibilities such as savings, bills and debt re-payments. I'm never ashamed to tell you my worst money mistake as a teenager. The mistakes I want you to avoid.

Throughout my teenage and college life, I made huge mistakes when it came to budgeting. My worst mistake was when I spent $100 a month on fast foods for me and my friends. That may or may not sound ridiculous to you but it does to me, now that I know better. Each semester, my three friends and I would go out to eat. We'd take turns paying for everyone. I'd spent $100 on food in just 20 school days. Instead, I could've developed a habit of buying lunch at school or brought a lunch box and used my parents' money wisely. So essentially, I would waste $100 a month, or $500 in a semester by going out to eat every day. It was a major budgeting mistake. I urge you now, my daughter, from the bottom of my heart not to make this mistake. I could have saved all that $100 a month and could have afford myself a small car when l completed my studies. I am going to share some more budgeting tips to avoid the mistake l did and to help you successfully maximize the money you make.

Understand your income

Making money as a teenager is a great feeling but you'll learn soon enough that what you're promised and what you actually earn are different things. For example, when you get a pay slip, you need to know how much money you'll get both before and after taxes also known as separating gross income from net income. As a result, you will know how much money you really get from any wages you have earned. Once you determine that, add up any income makers which will not require tax deductions such as tips, gifts, bonuses or allowances. On the safe side, in case these figures vary over time, add up the income you received over the last few months, then divide that total by the number of months to determine your average income and plan from there.

Project your expenses

Now comes the not-so-fun part: making a budget. Like your income, layout whatever potential expenses you have coming your way for the month in question. Include mobile phone costs, food and drink, grooming costs (haircuts, clothes, makeup, etc.), or any other living expenses. Some of those expenses will differ over time. Having a separate budget for each month will help reduce the stress. One of the easiest ways to manage your spending is by having a spending list which you can always go through each time when you have an income.

Less is more: spend wisely

You're growing into a stage of your life where you will meet new friends, have eye-opening social experiences and buy yourself things you've always wanted. While spending your own money for the things you dream of is a nice feeling, it can leave nightmarish effects on your financial future if mismanaged. Borrowing money can be a blessing and a curse at the same time. When you turn eighteen you will qualify to have your own clothing accounts and borrowing. A clothing account or loan is a ready-made solution to help you pay for something when you're a little short on cash and also taking clothes on credit. You will have to know that you still have to pay them off and if you aren't making a quality salary, it can be a tough task. If you don't need to use a card when going out, leave it at home. Clothing accounts or loans are more for credit score in case when you want to make significant purchases, not necessarily for those designer shirts or dresses you've been eyeing through shop windows. Having a card or borrowing money feels empowering, it can give you too much power, which can lead to you hanging your head in shame as you come back to me as your parent for a bail out. I'm not raising you that way. I don't want to one day sit with you with debt collectors in our midst. Never!

Save for it if you really want it!

At fifteen you're pretty much an adult in training. During this training stage, you will learn how to become more self-reliant and be able to spend your money on what you need. This letter is one such training module I have prepared for you. Establishing long-term saving goals helps you manage future expectations for those major life goals you wished when growing up. Whether it be your first car, a place of your own or to start your own business, you need the vision to set those goals in motion.

Keep earning

No matter how old you are, there is no such thing as "too much work". If you have the right physical and mental abilities, take on as many income-builders as possible so that saving becomes a natural practice. Picking up odd jobs along the way helps. Whether it's babysitting, tutoring children, taking on small jobs will keep income flowing. If your neighbor or friends are too busy (or lazy) to do these menial tasks, they'll look for help and you can make some easy money. Just let mom know where you will be and what you will be doing.

Any part-time jobs also help. The more you keep yourself active, the more opportunity you'll have to reach the earning potential you seek.

Take advice, lots of it

Look, you might have that bit of youthful pride that makes you think you know everything and questions what adults tell you. "What do they know? They're flawed people too." Yes, they are, and as one of them, I have already personally admitted some of my flaws, but they've been through the peaks and valleys of financial management or lack of it and can guide you.

As your parents we are a good first source. We can advise you on how to make the most of any allowances or income you get so that you don't have to beg us for cash at every turn. In addition, reading helps a lot as well. Search for personal finance books and read something every day.

Learn about inflation

As I mentioned previously, costs vary over time. What cost $100 a few days ago may cost almost double tomorrow due to inflation. Inflation is a steady increase in prices of goods and services and it gives a clearer indication of why you have to pay higher costs going forward. For example, here in Zimbabwe the history of hyper-inflation has taught us never to keep our money in the local currency because it will lose value. So, everyone changes it into foreign currency as soon as they are paid in local currency.

Divide and rule

Now my daughter if you are not sure how much money you should set aside for expenses and personal financial goals, you are not alone. Many people including adults like me struggle with that. However, you don't need to be a mathematics major in order to do that but a basic knowledge on percentages will surely help. You are doing your 'O' Level and I'm sure these are common mathematics exercises you encounter frequently in your studies, so I'm not worried about you solving that on your own.

I know that as a teen, the typical thing to do is to blow all your money on trivial items or on junk food. I know it because I've been there. I was once a teenager like you. However, there's a better way of budgeting your money. It's called the 50/30/20 rule. I'm sure you've heard of it but just in case you haven't, experts suggest that you spend 50% of your money on your needs, 30% on your wants and 20% on your savings. This is a good rule of thumb for most people; however, it does apply a little differently to teens like you. You don't need to spend 50% of your money on your needs.

Your dad and I have not yet negated our responsibility to provide for most of your needs. You are a member of the digital generation and I know that the most necessary expenses for you come in the form of internet data and phone payments. However, as teens you tend to spend most of your money on your wants like food, fashion, and accessories. Though there are exceptions since as teens you don't have to pay for rent, groceries and other expenses because as parents we cover them. Against this background, to you my daughter, whatever you are going to get as income, I suggest a 30/30/40 rule. 30% Needs: phone, car, insurance, groceries, other bills, 30% Wants: clothes, fast food/junk food, electronics, accessories, and 40% Savings: savings account, emergency fund, college savings, retirement savings, investing.

As I said before, this is to equip you and doesn't mean we won't be doing our parental duties. Sometimes, your needs may be way higher than 30% of your income and there's not much you can do about that. Maybe you tell mom about it and mom is not very much forthcoming. If that's the case, lower your wants as much as you can, and take the rest out of what you would put in savings. Sticking to set figures allows you to develop discipline with your money so you won't hear me nagging you about why you spend so much because I will be monitoring you.

Growing up is all about making tough decisions and the earlier you make them, the better your future will look. Money doesn't grow on trees, but a stable financial outlook stems from good decision making. Through saving, understanding your money and these other great tips, budgeting as a teenager will be much easier.

Chapter 6

Now as I come closer to the end of my letter, let me recap what I have been stressing all along. I want you to tell me the best topic or piece of advice this long letter has given you. Is it any of the following?

-Money personalities and what they entail with your spending habit and how you handle your finances.

-Values and beliefs affecting your relationship with money.

-Types of money beliefs or money scripts

-Re-shaping your money memory to new habits to boosts financial freedom.

-How to earn with no capital and how best to use your talents to earn money.

-What to do with the money you earn as a teenager, how to best manage the money.

-What is meant by budgeting and saving money, ways to make money work for you.

Well, my wish is that all this makes a composite piece of advice to you where the subtraction of each piece will affect the rest. Now let me give you five ways to stay on top of your finances as you get into the adulthood world.

Money matters make it count.

It is my fervent wish that you will be able to learn to deal with financial decisions you face everyday. Most of us may think of financial decisions in terms of big decisions such as when to buy a house and how to save for retirement. I emphasize that many small decisions have financial consequences. For example, when it's lunchtime, you need to choose whether you will eat lunch at the restaurant or have your packed lunch. You must always try to experience success in trying the ideas such as being able to save money by budgeting and finding alternatives to shopping. Remember what I told you on budgeting and saving earlier on.

Always think about the future

You should never look at saving money as a burden. Saving money must be one of your priorities. This is difficult even for most adults to grasp, but it is, without a doubt, one of the most important lessons I'm teaching you in this note. Even if you have made mistakes and have no extra money now, you can become a saver. Though an early start is helpful, saving at any time will put you on the right path to a better financial condition. I will have to add this again so that you can just start the saving habit NOW.

Learn to recognize wants and distinguish them from needs. One of the ways that will make you be the leader of your finances is to be able to identify and consider all options available. Comparing a premium brand to house brand at the grocery store, for example, can show you that you may want a certain (heavily advertised) brand, but you need certain foods. I know how you young girls fall for media hyped brands. You must be able to control your money, or the money will control you. The key is to understand that it is right to splurge occasionally, as long as your financial obligations have already been met.

You must be creative with your money subject

Creativity promotes outside-the-box thinking. It will also help you make sounder decisions. With the way life keeps getting more and more expensive as we grow older, it is imperative that as a teen you learn to approach financial problems with an open mind.

Understand how to manage debt

I am not a big fan of borrowing and debts but let me just add this just in case you find yourself in debt. I however wish you will follow mom's way of doing things. All the same, you must understand that there are two types of debt, Good and bad debt.

Good Debt versus Bad Debt

As a Teen you need to learn about different kinds of debt. While all liabilities need to be repaid as a part of every budget, one type of debt can move you forward while the other holds you back.

"Good debt" is money you borrow that helps you reach your goals. Student loans can be considered good debt if they help you earn a degree leading to employment. The amount of good debt someone takes can also be a real problem. As a teen you should consider all of the options before taking out massive loans to your education or purchasing anything or even starting on a business.

You must try to avoid "bad debt" at all costs. Bad debt usually carries high-interest rates and is often used to purchase our wants instead of needs. Borrowing money too often from family and friends or taking a loan from those people who offer high interest short term loans can put you in a cycle of debt that's hard to recover from.

By all cost learn to avoid debt, learn to live within your means and save for that item you want. I emphasize this because it is one of the big mistakes I made in my teens. I would borrow money to buy clothes, to impress people I don't even like, which caused me lot of trouble and which almost caused me depression. Please avoid that.

In signing off my letter I want to pose a question: So how much should a teenager save? Or you may ask yourself, "What should I save up for as a teenager?" If you want a big-ticket item such as a new tablet or something else, you'll need to cover the initial cost and any other expenses. Only you know if something is worth it or not. Being a smart money manager means that you can delay instant gratification so that you can build your savings. It may not be easy but when your bank account grows, you may have enough funds to pay for something special and still have money left over.

I hope you enjoyed this long and winding money letter and all the tips I have offered. I love you my daughter and I want to help you grow up and become a financially independent adult. Once again, Happy Birthday!